Trail Talk

Embark on a Rugged Journey Towards Mindfulness and Freedom

By Tyler Heath

splatter
publishing

This book is dedicated to those seeking peace in an anxious world.

CONTENTS

ACKNOWLEDGMENTS

To Mom, Alyssa, Rich, Felicia, Jenna, and J. Michelle Davis this book could simply not have been created with out your efforts. I am forever grateful.

Forward

"Not all who wander are lost."
-J.R.R. Tolkien

The End

It's been eight days since I ended my journey on the Appalachian Trail. The adjustment has been crazy; I feel like an outsider plopped back into to an old reality. Everything is moving so fast, and I feel so slow.

I look back at my journals from the trail in hopes of discovering some wisdom that might help in this difficult transition, but at first glance, I find none. It's hidden underneath my piss poor grammar and trash handwriting.

As I read further on, I become overwhelmed with a deep sense of gratitude. I end up completely losing sight of my search for wisdom and I ask one question instead; "How is this my story?"

It's hard to imagine. I was once shy, conservative, and meek. Now I'm changed.
It baffles me.

But these are my stories, and this is who I am.

My name is Tyler Heath. I'm like you; music, food, sports, family, events, jobs, school, friends, they all take part in forming my identity. But also like you, there's more to me than what meets the eye. The roots, the reasons, the *why* behind the things I identify with are harder to see.

My roots are Jesus. Centering my soul in faith has led me into a purposeful love of life worth sharing with others. Attempting to live like Jesus has changed me for the better, but I have found in my past I cared more about changing others than myself.

There came a point when I realized I was attempting to give something I didn't actually have. Peace, hope, love, faith. I had some and God worked with the little I gave. But most of what I shared was knowledge. It's hard to give peace, hope, love, and faith when I lacked it in my own soul.

After the AT, I have found myself in a much better place. A place of integrity and authenticity. Not perfection, but a place of mindfulness. **I'm okay with being okay, and I feel comfortable sharing about it**. I have dug deep and worked hard to clearly express the truth I feel within.

The layout of this book is short chapters that contain a journal entry from my time on the trail, followed by a life lesson derived from that experience.

My hope is that the lessons I learned will activate your heart, which might activate your mind, and finally activate change to make this world better.

The Beginning

My first experience with the AT was on a road trip when I was 16 years old. I was on my way to NYC and was crossing over Bear Mountain Bridge when I noticed a sign. It read, "AT: Historic Trail Crossing" I asked my mom what the sign was talking about. She explained that "AT" stood for Appalachian Trail, the 2,000-mile long hiking trail from Georgia to Maine. I looked and saw a rugged couple crossing the bridge with a big rucksack and hiking poles. I clearly remember saying to myself, "What dumbass would ever do that?" To someone who had never hiked before, it seemed painful and boring. Who would want to walk that far and for that long?

Little did I know, six years later that "rugged looking dumbass" crossing the bridge would be me.

The AT goes through fourteen states and is the most iconic long trail in the world. It is rugged, rocky, and rooty. I walked up epic mountains and eventually down them. I waded through rivers and creeks. I walked through towns and down roads. I climbed up, over, and under boulders. I dodged rattlesnakes, tics, and bears. I walked when it was sunny, cloudy, snowy, and rainy. I slept in shelters, tents, and hammocks. I drank water from streams and ate just about anything I could get my hands on. I barely showered, and I always smelled. I met foreigners, M.D.'s from Harvard, homeless people, ex-Marines, marine biologists, the mid-30's-life-crisis-crowd, preppy millennials, and the whole shebang. And I witnessed some of the most incredible sunrises, sunsets, and vistas this world has to offer. But at the end of the day, the trail is impactful because of its length.

It's a long ass trail. People who complete the whole trail usually take four to five months to do so. I hiked for around three months and went from Pennsylvania to Maine, and then Pennsylvania to Southern Virginia. In AT lingo, this style of a hike is called a "flip-flop."

But here's where shooting the shit ends and authenticity begins: Why did I hike the trail?

Here's part of a journal entry I wrote four months prior to starting this journey:

2/2/18: Harrisburg, PA

- *I want to be still. This world and culture moves fast. I am a product of this speedy American way and despite the benefits, I carry too much anxiety. I need to somehow let it go.*
- *I hold onto a lot of pain. Shame, hurt, and brokenness are some of the burdens I carry. I need a place where I can take time and heal.*
- *I need to get out of my context. I follow culture and others too much. I want to follow my soul and Jesus more.*

- *I want to actually reflect. Where have I been and where am I going? And what are the driving forces under all of these decisions I'm making?*
- *I need new perspective with how I view the world and myself. One that can help me cast a clearer vision for my future and view myself in a better light.*
- *I'm too comfortable. I need to face fears and push myself to move forward.*
- *I love the trail. Simplicity, trials, peace. The trail is those beautiful words blended together.*

Ultimately, my spirit was unsettled and unrooted. But I wanted to heal. **I wanted to be alright when the circumstances were all wrong.**

However, there was one seemingly obvious goal I forgot to add: finish the trail. For a competitive spirit like me, how could I forget the most important part?

But maybe, just maybe, the impact wasn't in the accomplishment but rather the journey.

Welcome to my journey.

Solitude

"If you're lonely when you're alone, you're in bad company."
-Sartre

Day 86 Journal Entry: Shenandoah, Virginia

I'm still on edge. Last night it was growing dark and before going to bed I posted up next to my tent ready to take a piss. I heard a noise to my right, but didn't react because I thought it was just a squirrel. Then I heard it again. I look...

And yell, "HOLY SHIT!"

There is a black bear standing on its hind legs, eight feet away, staring at me. Luckily, there were some people near who helped me scare it away. I'm thankful to say the least.

That marked the 13th bear I have seen in three days. This is my survivor story haha.

It poured last night, all day today, and now my stuff is soaking wet. To make matters worse, the last human I saw was when that bear freaked me out during my piss. I arrived at the campsite tonight, set up my tent, tore off my kicks, and threw my crocs on.

Most importantly, my bear bag toss was impeccable tonight. I'm impressed. Backpacking is not that hard… it's just walking. But I admit, I'm getting damn good at weird things, such as throwing bear bags.

Anyhow, I'm all alone again tonight, hence the long journal. I'm next to a stream so it's quite peaceful. I'm tired and ready for bed after a solid 27-mile day. It's weird; I've been hiking alone for the last 30 days, and it doesn't feel that bad because I see others and have short conversations a few times a day. But since I have seen more bears than humans lately, and it's pouring rain, dark, and foggy, I admit it's quite lonely.

Zzzz (6 hours later)

I just woke up.

I think I could have just died. It is now three am and I am completely awake. A nearby lightning strike must have started a small rock slide above me.

Those rocks tumbling down the mountain might have been the loudest noise I have ever heard. "Well this would be a crazy way to go," I thought.

Life Lesson:

Before this trip, I thought of solitude as situations like the one I described or maybe Alaskan Bush People. I thought of fellows like Ralph Waldo Emerson, philosopher-esque people who sit in the woods, smoke blunts, write weird poetry, and meditate.

I think originally I just misinterpreted the definitions of silence and solitude.

Silence describes the setting I'm in.

But solitude defines not what surrounds me, but what is within me.

I've been in quiet rooms and parks, but my mind, heart, and soul are in a thousand other places. I've sat in coffee shops and been a yogi, yet my mind is racing when it should be at peace.

A.K.A. I have a "loud ass soul."

I walked through twenty years of life consistently putting myself in silent settings expecting change. But I never attempted to deal with the actual problem: the inner noise.

In a world full of noise, silence and time alone are important. But I now believe, in a world full of hurt, solitude is what is necessary. It sucks. It's hard. But it's necessary.

For me, the trail was a step of bravery where I finally decided to enter solitude and journey through my brokenness.

I knew the answer to most of my inner battles. With WebMD, self-help articles, and religious books, it's not that hard to find answers. **But because we live in a world where solutions are one click away, we forget healing is a process, not an answer.**

This was my process:

First, I had to show up every day willing to work through my shit and let God love me. It was easy to beat myself up since I would fail daily, but this shame was quite detrimental to the process. If God does not shame me, I should not shame me.

Next, I had to name my brokenness. I couldn't defeat an enemy if I didn't know what enemy I was fighting against. I learned to call out my anxieties and fears daily so I could react and heal.

Then, I would ask God for help in learning to react differently. Usually when my imperfections are exposed, all hell breaks loose. Anger, cynicism, arrogance, anxiety, and bossiness all enter the playing field when I lose control. There are easy ways to cover and numb this pain. I have my fixes; I have tried different things, but the hurt keeps returning. I forget that I am loved, and instead of internalizing that truth, I search elsewhere to find it.

Changing the rhythms of a soul takes time. And it hurts. Prior to the trail, I was only just covering my cuts with Band-Aids. I would temporarily mask the pain of anxiety and never deal with the actual wound. **I never became okay with just being okay.** The temporary stuff I would seek for healing was just that: temporary.

This is why I invited God into the process of solitude. I couldn't fix myself since I was broken in the first place. I wouldn't expect a wounded soldier to reattach their leg and stitch themselves; I would expect a doctor to do that. For most of my life I would rely on myself through this process when all along God said He/She would lead me through it. Yes, I need to take part, but Doc is going to do the heavy lifting.

Lastly, I had to keep showing up. Day after day, mile after mile.

I entered this process of solitude literally and figuratively on the AT, and it changed my life.

Comfort Zones

"A ship in a harbor is safe, but that's not what a ship is built for."
-Unknown

Day 19: Salisbury, Connecticut

"I'm in a hospital right now. It feels like I'm in the movie "The Hangover" when the dude wakes up in the most-out-of-this-world scenario after everything was going just fine.

24 hours ago, I had just finished a 24 mile day. I was a bit tired, but life was good. My trail legs were starting to kick in and I felt strong.

But shit hit the fan at three a.m. I woke up and was about to explode out of both ends. I bolt to the privy (aka a toilet seat in the woods) only to soon realize I didn't have enough toilet paper to get the job done. And living up to my self-

proclaimed nickname of "Big Rock Guy," I grab some rocks and leaves to complete the task.

I played that fun game, running to the privy, for the rest of the night. When my friends nearby woke up in the morning and saw my face, they said, "You literally look green."

From seven a.m. to twelve p.m. I laid in the fetal position moaning. I literally couldn't move. I was dehydrated and stomach cramps kicked in. I attempted to drink the Gatorade my friends gave me but instantly puked it up. I needed to get out of the woods.

I called a hostel to pick me up at the closest road. It was only two miles away on flat ground; it was possibly my two hardest miles on the trail. I fell and pulled my quad on the way, forcing me to use my poles as crutches. As I laid down on my pack waiting for my ride, I picked up my eyes and noticed that a tick was halfway in my arm.

I arrived at the hostel and showered. All of my clothes had puke contaminates on them, so I ended up borrowing some from the chick who owned the hostel. Those tight jeans made my ass look nice. Very kind of her.

At this point I still hadn't been able to keep even water down, so I hadn't drunk in over 20 hours. I called my sister and since she couldn't calm me down, I called my mom. After telling me to go to the hospital more than enough times, I finally conceded.

I pulled up to the hospital via the taxi and "splat." My phone shatters on the ground. It was unusable. I literally said out loud talking to myself, "There is officially nothing else that could go wrong today."

I said "Hello" to the lady at the front desk and she started freaking out for me to get in a wheelchair. I was trying to tell her I was fine. But by the look on her face, I obviously didn't look fine.

And that leaves me here, 24 hours of hell later, journaling and watching the Warriors game from my hospital bed. I have the Norovirus, a tick bite, a pulled quad, and a shattered phone. Hell of a day. Hell of a day."

Life Lesson:

I firmly believe misery makes memories. Now I don't purposely go after agonizing events to produce memories, but I purposely seek uncomfortable situations for the sake of progress. I didn't want the Norovirus, a tick bite, or a shattered phone. But I pursued the AT, a journey way out of my comfort zone, for the opportunity to grow.

Putting myself in challenging environments always results in personal growth and strengthened faith. Through the trial, I either develop from my success or learn from my missteps; both sides of the spectrum produce growth.

I believe God wants me to become my truest self, a refined version of my current self.

The process of refining occurs in uncomfortable situations and is therefore where growth lies, and God dwells.

In entering difficult circumstances, I often lack control. I have to face my fear and walk into the unknown of the journey, trusting it's going to work out even if I'm unsure it will. And that is the essence of faith: trusting in something greater than myself that makes all things work out.

When I start to live in that peace, I want more of it, perpetuating the deepening of my faith. I start to make decisions that are less reliant on myself and more dependent on God.

I become confident in God and present within the journey, shaking pride at its core and leaving fear in the dust. Events in my life such as hiking the AT, not having a job, family problems, etc. can't shake me since I do not fear the unknown. Instead, I trust. I take faith.

Faith, more peace, less anxiety, no fear; that is where my confidence is rooted. I'm called to face my fears, trust it will work out, and enter the unknown. And I happen to believe that facing my fears in uncomfortable settings is exactly where God awaits me and the journey of faith begins.

Hope

"If we could read the secret history of our enemies we should find each man's life sorrow and suffering enough to disarm all hostility."
- Henry Wadsworth Longfellow

Day 25 - Massachusetts

Tyler, what if I told you today will be your hardest day? Will you look back and agree? Not the 24 hours of hell you experienced a few days ago, not the 30 mile day you put in last week, not re-pulling your quad and crutching two miles to camp, but today. Today is your most valiant day.

Today I have to sit still for the first time. I have been camping for five days since I got out of the hospital and re-pulled my quad. I had company the first few days, but now I'm alone.

I can't fill my soul with accomplishment because I literally can't move. I can't fill my soul with planning because every fucking plan I make gets ruined out here. I can't run, and all I want to do is run, run away from all of this anxiety built up over the years.

Fuck this.

And yet I recognize that I came out here for this very moment.

To face my fear. To be still.

Life Lesson

I was stuck. I had multiple panic attacks those three days, and it was miserable. I felt like I was living in my worst nightmare, a life where I couldn't move and couldn't plan.

One of my original goals of hiking the AT was to be still. Writing this was an error on my part, I somehow forgot that you can't be still if you're hiking twenty miles a day. Yes, I'm a dumbass.

But it was during this circumstance that I realized it wasn't my physical state that needed to be still, it was my soul. And maybe this combination of everything going wrong, not being able to physically run away from my inner anxiety, being in nature, and being alone, was a setting preplanned to allow me to cope with my anxiety.
Hope broke this debilitating cycle. Hope gives me the ability in difficult circumstances to see the light at the

end of the tunnel. **I trust that it's going to be okay, even though it's not okay now.**

When I come to the end of myself, I rely on God to work it out. My weakness turns into dependence. I tap into the strength of an infinite being stronger than myself. I allow God to become involved in my trials to turn me into my truer self.

But trials still hurt, and I often cower. I seek comfort instead of seeing the trial through. I lose vision of better days or a truer self, and I take the easy way out.

I discount the value of hope, and I replace it with comfort.

Which is why I don't reread that story in pain but in thankfulness. I am thankful for the trial, and I am thankful for God, friends, and family consistently telling me **"it was going to be okay."**

The trial was an opportunity of a lifetime, and their words of hope gave me the strength to get through it. They helped me envision greater things to come when I couldn't see past the clouds of my own hardship.

When I'm stuck, I typically say, "screw this" not "I need help." I attempt to act tough by handling the situation myself. I end up failing and creating another deep wound within, unbeknownst to the world.

My friend Nate says it best, "People around me are in a lot more pain than I realize, and I'm in a lot more pain than people around me realize."

I need to be better at accepting hope in the midst of my pain. And I need to be better at giving it to others in the midst of theirs.

Everyone is going through something. Everyone could use a little hope.

Perspective

"If you change the way you look at things, the things you look at change."
–Dr. Wayne Dyer

Day 31: Vermont

"I'm just chilling on a vista, thinking. 75% of my time out here I question why the hell I'm out here, and the other 25% of the time it all makes sense. It's the 25% moments like now, where society and culture can't cloud my vision, and I can see clearly.

Do I live with purpose? I don't think I have. Meaningless hustle and bustle has disguised itself as purpose in my life. And what about success? I'm a product of American culture. I have no shame in pursuing greatness, but out here it all looks so different. A life of busyness and a few successful moments. I have called this purpose in my life.

It's scary to think about. That I could have gone so far in life chasing something I didn't know I was chasing, something so meaningless."

Life Lesson:

New settings, specifically uncomfortable ones, are the places God upgrades my prescription lenses. I can finally trash the old ones and wear something that allows me to see.

Hiking the trail was an upgrade to my lenses. On this uncomfortable journey I gained a new perspective, and I started to ask better questions: questions that could be wrestled with and didn't have a straight answer. Because of this I've learned more about myself than ever before.

What actually relaxes me? What gives me energy? What am I pursuing? Where am I going? What is my purpose? Who do I care about? What do I care about?

Since I never attempted to work through these questions, I failed to discover my purpose.

In my past, a lack of direction made it difficult to live in the moment. Events, emotions, and relationships passed by without my notice. Moments that were supposed to draw me towards something divine and good. Moments worth experiencing and completely available for the taking. But these moments were lost. I missed out.

It's like climbing a mountain and getting to the top only to realize nothing fulfilling was actually there.

And instead of changing how I climb the mountain, I just put my head down and attempt to climb an even bigger mountain. My thought is that the bigger one must have what I'm looking for, but they are the same.

My life often looks like me hiking these mountains. I busy myself all day in the pursuit of a future successful moment. Only to realize when I get to the top I pursued a moment, not the present and most definitely not the journey. The pursuit of success and busyness had me future oriented**. I was looking ahead for something that was available now.**

Jesus was called, Emmanuel, meaning "God with us." Purpose, healing, and peace are available in the here and now. The divine is available in the here and now. God is with us.

Day 31: Continued

"As I digest this thought, I'm overwhelmed with emotion. Tears run down my cheeks. The pursuit of busyness and success has defined so much of my life. Freedom from this process feels so right. Journeys for vistas define my love of hiking, while perspective shifts define my pursuit of faith. Entering uncomfortable settings and wrestling with tough questions has liberated my experience of the present. Perspective shifts are changing how I see myself and the world.

Anxiety

"Peace. It does not mean to be in a place where there is no noise, trouble, or hard work. It means to be in the midst of those things and still be calm in your heart."
-Unknown

Disclaimer: My anxiety is not your anxiety. Every case is complicated and difficult. Please do not take my words as a broad answer to all anxiety problems out there.

Day 30: Green Mountains, Vermont

"I stopped at a shelter around mile 20 today and considered calling it a day. Some college students told me thunderstorms were coming but encouraged me to keep moving since they wouldn't hit until later.

Later just happened to mean one mile later. And before I knew it I was walking through a torrential downpour. I was pissed!!

At that moment I started clenching my jaw and grinding my teeth. Anger consumed me.

I passed a hiker, "who wasn't walking fast enough" and initiated a rude conversation with him. Only after passing this man did I realize he wasn't the one with the problem. I was.

I wanted him to be pissed off like me so that I could validate my own bad attitude.

I didn't just expect this, I wanted it.

Life Lesson:

I look back at this journal in disgust. I let rain give me anxiety. I was literally getting anxious over rain. And I didn't just internalize it, I attempted to share it with others.

Because the anxiety I carry, I give to others.

The weight on my shoulders is always transferred to those around me.

As someone who longs to impact the world, I often fail for this very reason. Our world needs more peace, yet I give it anxiety.

Anxiety is a tangible thing. It affects me mentally, spiritually, and physically. In the moment, my body is slumped in disappointment, my attitude shot from anger, and my soul riddled with impatience of my uncertain future.

Its source is different for all people. For many it's the big game, public speaking, planning a huge life event, etc. that is the source of anxiety in their life. It's the fear of messing up that has them going crazy.

For myself it's the opposite. **I receive anxiety from sitting still.** When I have zero input and everything is out of my control, I freak out. And here is where the paradigm lies: somehow I carry anxiety from the things I can't actually control, and those that I can control, I don't.

The way society works today, I feel like I have the ability to command everything around me. Technology is deceptive. It gives me power, but it doesn't make me god. It might be able to tell me the weather, but I am not one click away from ending a rain storm. I have to admit that there are things out of my capacity to perform.

But admitting is not enough; I must actually let go. God wants me to give up these uncontrollable situations. Jesus was the center of God's plan to free this world of anxiety. He was God in flesh, handling the shit I usually put on my own shoulders. By trusting that God will actually come through, my soul becomes rooted. No longer do I have to ride the emotional roller coaster uncontrollable settings bring forth; rather, I can be at peace and thrive in all circumstances.

Through my time in the wilderness, I slowly redeveloped the habits of a peacemaker.

Day 30 Continued:

"Now I had a decision to make. I could walk through the rest of the rainstorm in anger and fear, full of anxiety, or I could not because the circumstance was not going to change. It was going to keep raining whether I liked it or not.

The only thing in this situation that was worth attempting to change was my own soul.

Today, I decided to trust that it was all going to work out, despite not being able to control the situation. What started as the worst rain storm I experienced on the trail, well, it turned out to be a fun walk in the rain. How about that?"

Awareness

"No one is as deaf as the man who will not listen."
-Jewish Proverb

Day 24: Connecticut
"I'm chilling with Ember this lazy morning. This man was that Dos Equis, Most Interesting Man in the world guy, I swear. A self-proclaimed "homeless man", he had a doctorate in Chemistry by the age of 26 when he realized he didn't like working for the "man" and decided to become a "doctor of the woods." A.K.A. he lived the next 20 years in the wilderness somewhere in California. He is the most rugged looking dude I have met on the trail. His fingers have no feeling. I discovered that this morning when he picked up a boiling pot of coffee with his bare hands and didn't react. He said he "gained this power" or nerve damage (however you look at it haha) from doing it every single morning the past 20 years.

We started talking, and eventually got into a conversation about spirituality. I could tell right away that I had put my guard up. I was thinking, "What the hell is this guy going to teach me about God?"
But I attempted to tear it down as quick as I could and listen. Our conversation centered around both of our life stories. Eventually he asked why I was camping and not hiking?

I explained to him my recent hospital visit, and how my return to the trail didn't go as planned after I reinjured my leg five miles in.

And His response was this: ***"Looks like the trail is trying to tell you something."***

Life Lesson:

Ember's final statement struck something deep within me. It was as if the light bulb turned on upstairs. The knowledge I possessed for years about the need to "slow down" somehow traveled the eighteen inches to my heart.

I used to struggle to be aware of divine experiences such as this one. Frankly, I used to struggle to hear God speak. I was waiting for some glowing angel guy to yell down from space and tell me all of life's answers. This never happened, so I gave up.

I was unaware of how God "speaks" which led to distance between myself and God.

Opportunities to experience something beyond myself went unrecognized.

But God does "speak" and God is never bounded by my expected channels of communication.

God spoke through a homeless person named Ember in the setting of the Appalachian Trail to tell me, "slow down." It was something I already knew and had written. But this time when I heard it, it was different. It was as if God was speaking directly to me.

God speaking does not mean an audible voice. God speaking is the ignition of a feeling within. The moment when what was unclear became clear, a moment rooted in something deep and something true, it is a moment where I don't just acknowledge the goodness of justice, hope, and love, but I feel it. It is the moment where I am called to action for something good, whole, and way beyond myself. My soul and heart have been activated.

God speaks daily, and I'm starting to recognize it. That feeling of truth and wholeness and goodness, that noble call to action is God speaking. I now listen to my soul and I attempt to act in courage, not by fear. The old St. Patrick prayer still rings true to this day, "God with us, God in us, God all around us." God speaks, and that "voice" is already within me and around me. I'm just now beginning to discover it.

Preconception

"The answer is that we are not helpless in the face of our first impressions. They may bubble up from the unconscious - from behind a locked door inside of our brain - but just because something is outside of awareness doesn't mean it's outside of control."
- Malcolm Gladwell

Day 8: New Jersey
I feel like a hypocrite on days like to today. My heart for social justice is tested, and I receive a failing grade. I don't "walk my talk."

Today, I walked by a guy named "Fox" who obviously would have enjoyed some company along the trail. But Fox looked rough to say the least. Tattered clothes, the stench of someone who hadn't showered in months, yellow teeth, and broken English drove my gut reaction to hike on without him.

I allowed my subconscious to convince myself that I was in a rush and would be better off alone, when in reality neither of those facts were true. My heart yearned to enter relationship, and yet my reaction was to deny it.

I often naturally make decisions I don't want to make.

Situations occur like this where I have an opportunity to pursue my calling, to "do justly, to love mercy, and to walk humbly with my God," but I miss out (Micah 6:8).

My truer self and a better world exists when I tap into this calling, and yet I often don't.

It's like I see the opportunity, and I feel it, but I miss it.

I miss out on hiking with friends like Fox. I miss out serving the greater good surrounding me.

Why?

Life Lesson:

Despite this head knowledge, it seems I tend to avoid "different" people in order to preserve personal comfort and safety. No doubt Fox smelled like trash and seemed a bit odd, but that should not have stopped me from entering relationship.

These false, snap judgments that drive my actions, reveal my preconceived bias.

Despite being designed for relationship, staying away from people I perceive to be "shady" such as Fox, rather then moving towards them is almost always my initial reaction. I have found that my bias is rooted in comfort.

By listening to my gut reactions I maintain this comfort, creating distance from anyone who threatens it. But by doing this I miss out on the beauty of relationships and lose touch with the connectedness of humanity.

I live with this binary mindset where I see people as either good or bad. Marvel movies are popular for the same reason; we connect with these ideas of good and evil.

But I don't have to see the world this way.

I live with bias, not because I see the bad in homeless guys on the AT, but because I refuse to see the good.

Jesus sees the good in all people, and I want to do similarly.
Changing this pattern has taken self-recognition and consistent attempts at humility.

I must recognize where my bias lies and when it is activated. And I must take every opportunity to elevate my view of humanity, by seeing others as greater than myself and acting accordingly.

The trail has helped me see through flaws, and enter the unknown of new relationships I would have never thought to have entered. I have started to see the greatness in people like Fox and it is changing my life.

Hospitality

"The only way to make a man trustworthy is to trust him."
-Henry L. Stimson

Day 75: Harpers Ferry, West Virginia

Today is the day: I'm attempting a 50-mile challenge. This encompasses getting out of PA, hiking through Maryland and ending in Harpers Ferry, West Virginia. The end goal is to accomplish this all within a 24-hour time period solely for the pride of being able to say, "I did it." (Not a good reason lol) I'm excited to get after it, but in order to prevent injury, I am going to treat it like a normal day and log throughout it.

My log:

Mile 0- Oatmeal/protein mix breakfast: Great night's sleep, I'm ready to go. Eight a.m. start time

Mile 5- Snicker bar break: Feeling solid, not buggy, and its good weather

Mile 10- Honey Bun break: This isn't bad at all, I wonder if I could do 75 today? That'd be dope!

Mile 15- Pop Tart break: This is honestly easy; I'm in the best shape of my life. Not sure why people hype this up?

Mile 20- Cliff Bar break: A little bored right now. This happens daily though. Going to throw in the ear buds and listen to an audible book.

Mile 25- Granola bar break: I've been doing this wrong. This is like a long car ride. I should call people to make sure I stay awake. (I have service today)
- I called and spoke to three friends the next five miles

Mile 32- Ten p.m. Dinnertime break: Two random hikers gave me a free hard cider and watched me eat a whole summer sausage and four tortillas. It's officially nighttime and dark out. Let the night hike begin…

Mile 36- Beef Jerky stick break: Ok I'm officially in new territory. This is the farthest I have ever hiked. That last mountain was tiring. Wow, I literally just yawned. I'm ready for bed!!

Mile 38- Filter water break: Ok my body hurts. This kind of sucks.

Mile 42- Sit ass down break: My feet are destroyed and everything hurts. This really sucks.

Mile 44- Honey Bun break: I am really glad I don't watch scary movies. It would suck walking in the pitch black, on a dark trail, with red eyes staring at me every few minutes if I thought I was going to be attacked. Also, I think this is one of the dumbest things I have ever done.

Mile 46- Fall over and lay in dirt break: I fell over and for a brief two minutes considered staying there and falling asleep. I took off my socks to check my feet and found six wretched looking blisters. My feet hate me, more than myself, and that's just hard to do at this point. Also, I just walked through my 53rd spider web of the night. I wonder how many spiders I have accidently swallowed?

Mile 49- Sit on ass break: Last three miles on flat ground have literally been hell.

Mile 50- Sit on ass break: Realized I have another mile up the hill and through town to get to my destination.

I am now journaling later in the day:

Mile 51- I arrived at my destination, the park bench. I was too muddy and gross to enter my tent so I attempted to sleep on the park bench, which didn't happen.

So here I am, sitting in the dark trying to tend to my feet when an elderly lady comes walking her dog by "my bench." My initial thought was, who the hell walks their dog at four a.m.? My second thought was to greet her, and so the conversation commenced.

Me- Good morning ma'am, how are you?

Sue- I'm well, How are you?

Me- Horrible (I was in a mood of being short and brutally honest)

Sue- How come?

Me- My feet are destroyed and I'm really gross, but can't sleep, and it's all because I'm a dumbass and hiked for 20 straight hours.

Sue- You come with me young man. We are going to get you cleaned up and get some food and beverage in you.

Me- Really???? Are you sure???

Sue- Yes

Life Lesson:

For hospitality to become a reality, one must create an opportunity for trust to take place.

Sue did exactly that. Sue invited me; a homeless, destroyed, gross looking millennial into her house at four am. She provided me with a meal, a shower, and some amazing conversation. She even let me chill at the house when she left to do her errands. It was a life giving experience and a memory I will never forget. I was taken from a moment of utter pain to one of pure joy.

In hindsight this friendship should have never happened. Sue had no reason to trust me. She did not know me, and my repulsive image did not scream "responsibility," nor did the setting make this a comfortable moment.

If hospitality is when people "have an open door" like Sue, I realized that by that same light, my door is often locked. Why is this?

It's because hospitality requires courage, and courage means letting go of comfort. Sue showed courage by letting a stranger into her home because she cared more about caring for me than preserving her comfort and safety.

Her radical act of hospitality revealed to me that my lack of hospitality is rooted in fear of losing that same comfort and safety. If hospitality is an "open door" mindset, fear rooted in self preservation is my "locked door" mindset.

Tangibly, I always lock my doors; mentally I'm restrictive of who I allow near me. These actions indicate that I am fearful of everyone and everything. Locking my doors and restricting relationships to preserve comfort is a norm in my life.

I will never actually find out if I can trust my neighbor in the first place if I don't give them a chance. When I lock my door, I ruin the opportunity for trust to take place.

If trust is developing relationships over time inside your house, hospitality requires cultivating the courage to initially open the door.

My initial reaction in life is to fear and keep the door shut. This is completely rational if I seek to serve myself most. But what if I sought to serve others first like Jesus said? What if I made trust the priority, kinship the purpose, and hospitality the game? Well, I think I know the answer. I would look more like Sue. And a world with more Sues is a world worth striving for.

Plans

"Life is to be lived, not controlled."
-Ralph Ellison

Day 37: White Mountains, New Hampshire
Today was one of those crappy weather days. We were hiking down North Kinsman Mountain in the Whites with heavy packs, tired legs, and weary souls. A treacherous mountain to climb in the first place, rainy conditions made it even more burdensome. Despite the difficult conditions, we had remained relatively positive as a group. That being until my sister slipped on a rock and destroyed her knee.

Life Lesson:

I have found in my life that 95% of the time I cry (childhood or adult life, yes I still cry) the surface level circumstance that initiated the sobbing is almost never the source of my tears.

I think the same applies to most. On the trail, my sister was in a lot of pain because of her knee, but I didn't believe it was enough to warrant tears. At least for her, since I know that she is tough as nails.

The knowledge of her injury was far worse than the physical pain of it.

Questions started popping around in her head as well as my own:

Would she be able to get down the mountain? Would she have to go to a hospital? Would she have to be by herself the rest of the trip? How will this affect us getting to camp on time? Will this ruin the trip for everyone else?

It doesn't matter if you are the injured person, a team member, or the leader. An anxious soul is an anxious soul, and it will always show up.

When my plans go wrong, I enter the unknown, and it's scary. My reaction is to plan.

Usually when I plan, my process is to ask new questions and attempt to answer them. This is a typical response; however, the problem arises in terms of the unknown. If a situation is outside of my knowledge or realm of experience, I have no answers to my questions. When I have no answers to my questions, I have no plans. No plans means an anxious soul. And so the rabbit hole of anxiety begins.

My usual, anxious response to similar circumstances is to freak out, try to plan, and become a bossy bitch. I live in a western world context where most are plan makers or plan fixers. My responses feel quite okay in comparison to those around me; however, just because it is a normal response, doesn't make it a good one. I live in a society where planning is the coping mechanism for plans gone wrong.

But what if God's plan for our lives was actually for us to stop planning our lives?

This point of view has started to change me. When plans have to be thrown away, I now trust. I put faith in God coming through and not myself. It gives me a tangible peace and produces a sturdier soul. I give the anxiety that I usually put on my own shoulders to a force that can actually handle it. I start to live, lead, and give peace, not anxiety.

I started this change on the AT. My first reaction when my sister was injured was not to freak out. I gave her a hug and said, **"It's going to be okay, it's going to be okay," because I trusted, it was going to be okay.**

Decisions

"The only choice you can't make is to choose alone."
-Proverb

Day 13: New York

"Tyler where's your "bear proof" bear bag?" another hiker asked jokingly.

My response, "Bear got it."

I laugh out loud when I replay this scenario in my head.

As a hiker, I am obligated to hang my food up in trees at nights to follow the "LNT" (Leave No Trace) rules put in place by the national park governing bodies. The purpose is to create a more sustainable ecosystem by keeping human food in our own stomachs and not the animals of the spaces we are invading.

I made the decision a few months prior in preparation for this scenario to purchase a "bear proof" food bag called an Ursak. That is in comparison to the other option, a normal bag you hang on a tree branch around 15 feet in the air with rope. Despite my experience using the second option, I wanted to make the "wise" decision, so I bought the Ursak.

Well I write all of that to say, I woke up this morning and my "bear proof" bag was taken… by a bear.

Life Lesson:

Don't falter for bogus marketing schemes. JK.

So, it turns out there is no such thing as a "bear proof" food bag.

The ironic part about my purchase was that I was "so sure" I was making the right decision.

I tend to be inherently cheap and risky, so I thought by doing the opposite I was being "wise."

Maybe it's my type A personality, but I realized that I actually like to make all of my decisions as if the one way is correct and the other is completely wrong.

Taking the time to think through the pros and cons of a decision is the essence of being wise. But at the same time the trail has helped me recognize that life is not all about being right and wrong. Life is much more than that, it's a journey of ups and downs where the right decision sometimes leads to a greater mess, and the wrong decision can actually save your life.

Life is not a bunch of black and white lines. There seems to be a lot of grey area, and I just seem to always be in the middle of it.

Unfortunately, I tie my faith to this faulty black and white worldview.

When I tell myself that a decision is either right or wrong, I then infer that God must then be on one side and not the other.

And this is the lie I believe: That God is on the side of whatever I judge to be the right side and not the wrong side.

I bear all of the weight of a big decision on my shoulders for no reason. **Whether I mess it up real bad or I hit the nail on the head, God is on both sides and therefore there is no reason to worry.**

I now put my faith in the fact that God is with us no matter the decisions we make, right or wrong. Black or white or gray. God is with us, always.

This gives me peace to make any decision because I know God is on either side of the spectrum, no matter the outcome. Hell, it even gives me peace when I make poor decisions that leads to a bear stealing all of my food, peace that lasts no matter the decision and no matter the outcome.

Reconciliation

"Behind every beautiful thing, there's been some kind of pain."
-Bob Dylan

Day 66: 100 Mile Wilderness, Maine

"So we woke up today. Can I even say that? Haha I'm honestly not even sure if Adam or I got more than an hour of sleep last night. It was so freaking gross and muggy which made it close to impossible to sleep, let alone breathe. Anyhow, we ate our oatmeal, which tasted more like the 'rambombs' we made last night, since we had never cleaned out our bowls. (Rambombs is Ramen noodles plus powdered mashed potatoes in a tortilla sandwich) So our oatmeal tasted like ass. And because we were not having a glorious sit down breakfast, we decided to get our own asses moving.

The problem was that the four straight days of hiking was finally taking a toll on Adam's knee. It probably only took us five miles before we realized his knee was wrecked. And to make matters worse, we found out a massive storm was going to hit in two days. Ipso Facto Adam and I had to hike 15 extra miles today to make sure we could summit Katahdin tomorrow (a day early.) That's a long time on tired legs, let alone a bad knee for Adam.

And so as it would happen often on the trail, pain seemed to blind the beautiful scenery we were walking in. Every step I'd feel a blister. Every root, Adam's knee would explode with pain. Every movement of our packs would pinch the raw skin around our hip belts, and oh the chaffing, don't let me get started. Today was rough. Every day is not like this, but today was. And it sucked.

But somehow it was all worth it today. Everything changed when we finished the hellish day. We got to Abol Bridge, bought beer and ice cream from the local convenience store, and just sat on the bridge overlooking the Penobscot River. It is here where we had an incredible view of Katahdin, the mountain we would summit the next day.

In that moment, the beer didn't taste like the Bud Light that it was, it tasted like a million dollar concoction my lips didn't deserve to touch. And the ice-cream, oh the ice-cream, it turned me on.

Life Lesson:

Shitty moments deemed "worth it" is my definition of reconciliation.

What made that moment different compared to every other time I had a cheap beer, average ice cream, and a decent view?

I'm convinced it was the reconciliation of that day. The pain from the trials faced earlier made me more appreciative of everything else in life. It was a moment when all that seemed to have gone wrong was somehow righted, and not just righted but worth it.

Reconciled moments are moments worth pursuing. Driving to the top of a mountain to see a vista is cool. Climbing that same damn mountain and putting blood, sweat, and tears into it just seems to make it that much better. It doesn't mean I don't wish it was easier or could have been done differently, but it does mean I recognize that it was all somehow worth it.

I don't know why things in this world are difficult. I don't know why bad things happen to good people, and I sure as hell don't know why some people have to experience disease, war, mental illness, prison, and famine.

I won't lie that brokenness often clouds my vision from having the faith to believe in good. But that is why I put my hope in Jesus, and the promise that God will reconcile it all.

A God that brought their own ass down from heaven, experienced the rough side of humanity, and conquered brokenness to reconcile the world we live in now.

God did it, so I can to take part in the reconciliation.

God promises that he/she won't just make it right for me but for the whole world. And it will not just be some flimsy, surface level, religious feeling to make me feel good, it will be a real and tangible hope I can see and feel in the here and now. It's these experiences that draw me towards a life with more faith. A life with less anxiety and more peace. A life that tastes like the beer and ice cream I had on Abol Bridge, like the best thing I have ever tasted or experienced, a life so worth living.

Mindfulness

"To be is to feel in the rush of the passing and the stillness of the eternal"
-Abraham Heshel

Day 93: Southern Virginia

Is it over?

I feel peace. I told it to Ry at lunch, "I literally feel like I'm breathing different." If that's not the definition of changing bad habits into good ones, then I don't know what is. A weight has been lifted off of my shoulders, and it is liberating.

I'm actually okay with being finished. Usually, I feel way more anxious over such a decision to "quit." But this feels like a true "Forrest Gump moment," where I'm on that grassy hill overlooking the George Washington Mountain Range in Virginia hearing a chorus yell, "You're free!"

Haha this is my decision. I'm free. I don't give a fuck about others' perception of me, the world's, or even my own. The roots to these perceptions of "failure" are flawed.

Identity in experiences, failure, success, or others is surface level. I'm over it and don't want it. I long for something deeper. I long for my soul to be sturdy and rooted in something greater than myself.

It's factual that most come to the point of, "Screw it, I just want to finish this trail." Old me says, "Hell yeah!" New and changed me says, "What's the point?" Especially if I'm going to be uprooting my own soul by chasing this deeply flawed longing for satisfaction in my own success.

I can't help but believe that the personal capstone to my success on this journey is in the "failure." Living out freedom. Living in it. Yes, living in it. That's all I wanted out of this, to experience God's love, grace, and peace. And not just talk about it. But be it. Feel it. Live it.

I sit here tonight and say, "Damn God, you performed a miracle in me."

Life Lesson:

Can I be okay with being okay?

I know I can because I experienced the freedom of living this mantra out.

Prior to the AT, I never thought it was attainable.

My identity was in too many things like family, friends, school, jobs, good food, athletics, religion, mainstream culture, and the list goes on.

All of these are good things, but none of them are powerful enough to drive my every decision or to root me in all circumstances.

On the AT, I stripped away everything I had ever put my identity in and came to the end of myself. The end of my ego was the beginning of something greater than myself, a relationship with the God of love, hope, and peace.

By ending my time on the trail, I let go of the last thing I put my identity in: the success of finishing the trail.

I quit, and what I found was not anxiety but peace.

My soul was rooted in something beyond itself and it felt good. And it lasts to this day.

When all in life is good
When fear is overwhelming me
When life sucks
When life is comfortable
When life is moving faster than I can keep up with
When people try to form my identity for me
When life is full of idle time
When culture says I'm different or wrong
When anxiety tries to overpower peace

I'm okay with being okay.

Afterward

"We don't realize that, somewhere within us all, there does exist a supreme self who is eternally at peace."
-Elizabeth Gilbert

May 2019 - One Year Post Trail:

My journey on the Appalachian Trail ended almost a year ago. And since then, a lot has changed.

As time moves forward, lessons learned in the past can fade into mere memories.

The stories and lessons within Trail Talk were powerful to me because they were raw, real, and present experiences. I wrote the core of Trail Talk while on the trail in a heightened state of emotional awareness. No, I was not smoking reefer; these experiences with peace were sincere.

But I'm also a realist, and the trail is in no way "real life." Self discovery can happen anywhere, but let's be honest, the trail draws people towards peace far more than the rush of life. Dealing with kids, a job, and to-do lists, are in no doubt distracting to anyone's pursuit of mindfulness.

It is within this "real life" context, I write to you now.

Trail Talk did not become a memory; Trail Talk became my "self-talk."

When anxiety comes daily, I'm more aware of it, and I am able to focus my energy on separating myself from it. I isolate anxiety, and I claim my independence from it. This freedom equates to peace. And this process is applicable anywhere, whether you're stuck on the trail with an injury or contemplating next steps after being fired.

Yesterday, I got canned from my job, and it stings.

Anxiety runs rampant with the implications that brings to the table. I long for security as my fears are amplified and my ego is depleted. It's in these moments of overwhelming hurt I recall the lessons I learned on the trail. Even when everything around me is not okay, I am okay.

Hardships and anxious circumstances will never leave. Today it's getting fired, and tomorrow it will be something else. But participating in this process helps me grow into my truest self regardless of the circumstance. My identity lies in love, not my success or failure.

Trail Talk was not about arriving at a destination. It was the beginning of a lifelong journey towards peace and mindfulness.

Made in the USA
Monee, IL
15 December 2019